FEARLESS LIVING

LIVING CONQUER YOUR FEAR, AND LIVE YOUR DREAMS

Published by Inprov, Ltd.
1203 S. White Chapel Blvd.
Southlake, TX 76092

Printed April 2008

Printed in the United States of America

FEARLESS LIVING

> GOD PLANTS VISION

There is a dream inside of you. That dream is your destiny, your call to greatness! God has blessed you with giftings and passions unique to your dream. He has not called you to be someone else, but to be you – the person He uniquely designed and loves.

What is your dream? Only you and God know it, and only you and God can make it come to pass. Unless you fully live out that dream, your life will fall short of God's purpose and you will never feel completely fulfilled.

Living out your dream won't be easy. You have an enemy who does not want you to reach your highest potential. He does not want you to bring glory to God or thrive in the joy of His favor.

To bring you down, the enemy uses a weapon strong enough to entrap you so that you cannot press on or reach higher. If you don't open your eyes and fight back, his attempts will steal, kill and destroy your dream (John 10:10).

Friends, the enemy's most crafty weapon against your dream is fear.

Yes, fear can bury your dream. When you allow fear to rule your life, the passion that calls to you from the depths of your heart will be pressed down and trapped. Unless you acknowledge your fear, look it straight in the face, you will never be free from its grip. Conquering fear will set your dreams free, and only then will your passion rise up within you to drive you to heights you never knew were possible.

To live your dream is to be fully alive. Don't let the enemy steal that life. Set your passion free. Run with endurance to be all that God created you to be. The only thing that stands in your way of fully pursuing your dream is fear.

So what are you afraid of? What fear has the enemy used to immobilize you? What will it take to finally be rid of the fear that keeps you from achieving your highest potential?

My name is Edward John, and I invite you on a journey to rediscover your dreams and identify the fears that hold those dreams prisoner. Go with me to a place where all your dreams can come true. Yes, such a place exists, and you can get there when you move forward with faith.

Travel with me through these pages, deep into your own heart, and you will discover that the road to a dream-filled tomorrow is marked with Fearless Living.

– Edward John

NAVIGATION

Friends, this book is the culmination of a journey for me. God has changed me, spoken to me and moved me to a place that I long for each and every one of you to discover and enjoy – the land of fearless living.

As you read through the pages of this book, you will discover keys and tools to help you on your journey to freedom. I want you to be able to take this journey with me as we wrestle through hard issues. On this journey, I encourage you with the truth and hope of the message God has given me to share.

In order to keep you engaged throughout the process, I have structured this book in a unique way. In each of the four major sections that present four specific fears (failure, loneliness, man and God), you will find pages with labels such as "Question" and "Echo." There are nine labels I will use for the different sections, all designed to keep you involved and connected.

Before you dive in, allow me to explain each of these sections:

> **INTRO** Many people are so used to living in fear that they don't recognize it as a crippling, enslaving disease. Each time I present a new fear, I will describe it so you can identify if it is a stronghold in your life that you need to confront.

> **QUESTION** Like I said, I want this book to be a conversation. Regularly throughout this process, I will ask you very pointed questions. While I may not be able to hear your answers audibly, you will answer them honestly in your heart. Don't breeze through these sections. Ponder the questions, pray through them and let the Holy Spirit highlight the truth that may be hiding deep within.

> **TRUTH** The enemy of progress is deception. If you feel stuck in life, like you can't seem to move forward in what God has called you to do, it is because somewhere along the way you have believed a lie. The truth of God from His Word is the only way to counter the enemy's attempts to destroy you with his lies.

> **TESTIMONY** Fearless living is a process that God has had me on for many years. I want to share the lessons and triumphs God has given me along the way to encourage you that His abundant life is within reach for all of His children.

> **KEY** In the fight to break free from fear, whether of failure, loneliness, man or God, I want to equip you with understanding attitudes or actions that will empower you in the daily battle to overcome.

> **ECHO** In my life, God often has to teach and remind me of the same lessons. The more He tells me about it, the more it sinks in. In "Echo," I want to bring it all together with some practical application points, so you will know how to take the next step toward fearless living.

> **SONG** God has blessed me with a ministry and passion for music. All of my songs commemorate a season in my life, a lesson God has taught me or a victory over sin and strife. I want to share with you the songs that have marked my journey in order to encourage you in yours.

> **PRAYER** Ultimately, God is the one who will set you free from your fears. His power, and His power alone, can break the chains that bind you. I invite you, as we tackle each fear, to join me in asking God for deliverance.

> **CHALLENGE** Finally, when I have finished talking to you about each individual fear, I will give you one last charge to take what you have learned and, by the power of God's Spirit, move forward without fear.

My heart's passion is for God to set you free from whatever is holding you back. I am so excited for you to turn this next page and press forward toward victory and freedom. Nothing, absolutely nothing, can compare with the life God has destined for you – one of complete trust in Him, intimacy with Him and adventure alongside Him as you accomplish all He has placed in your heart.

CHAPTERS

>>>

> 1 FEAR OF FAILURE

> 2 FEAR OF LONELINESS

> 3 FEAR OF MAN

> 4 FEAR OF GOD

> 5 FEARLESS LIVING

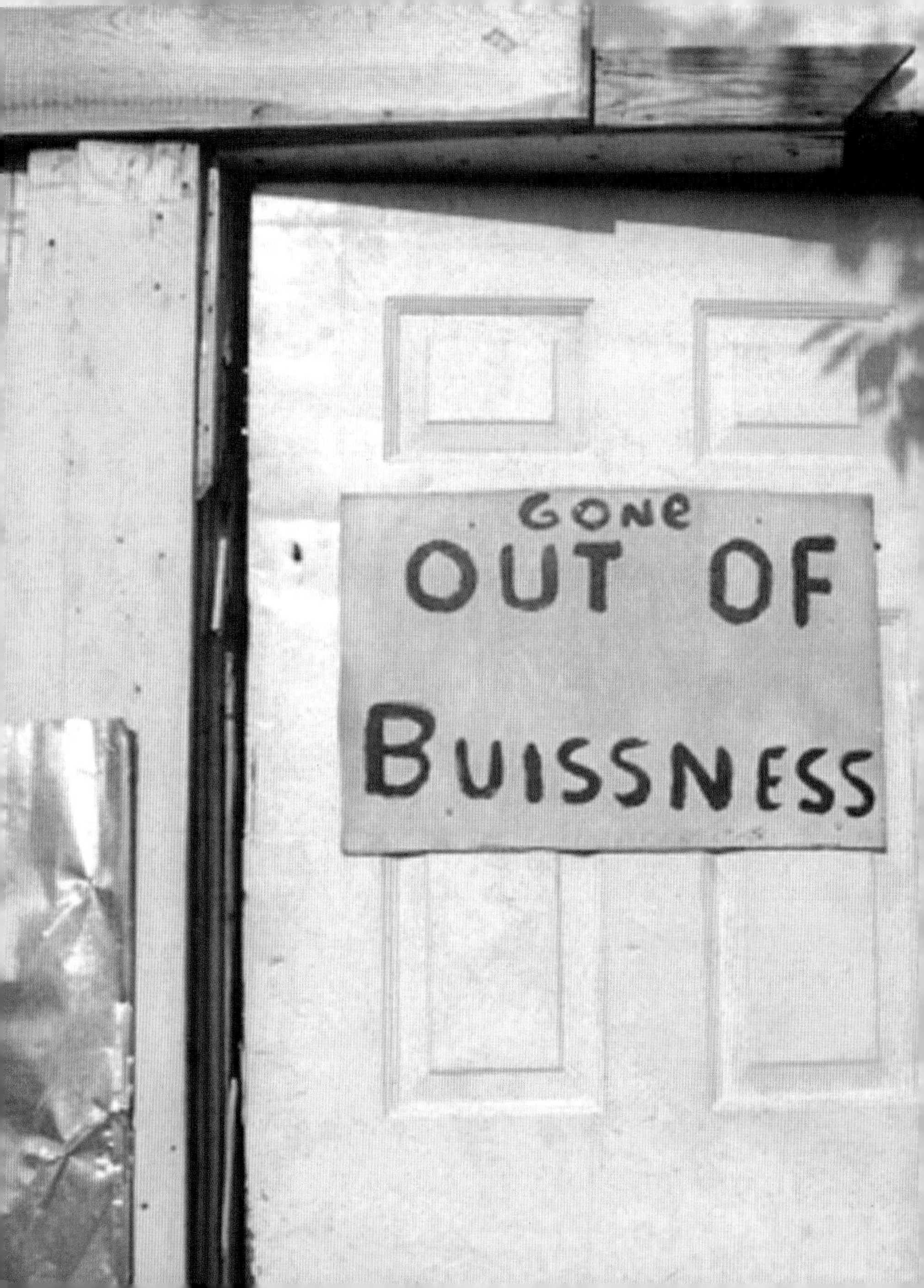
GONE
OUT OF
BUISSNESS

FEAR OF
FAILURE

FEAR OF FAILURE

INTRO >>>

 # AFRAID TO FAIL

God plants vision and potential in the hearts of all of His children. You have the desire, talent and passion to accomplish great things for Him. When He gave you these dreams, He did not set you up for failure, but for success. God wants the best for you!

Your potential is just dying to get out – that feeling inside that bubbles up, reminding you that you were created for something more. Maybe you are a housewife who wants to use your love for children to minister to your neighborhood. Maybe you are a young man with a passion for baseball or basketball. Maybe you are a career person with a dream to succeed at work.

Every one of us has vision and passion inside, but few of us let it out. What is stopping us? I'll tell you: We all have a natural tendency to shrink back from greatness because we don't think we can accomplish what is in our hearts. We are <u>afraid to fail</u>, and that fear keeps us from even trying.

From today forward, your life is like an empty canvas. Already, God has given you the dreams, giftings, opportunities and His loving support to create a masterpiece that glorifies Him. But unless you conquer that fear of failure, your life will fall short of what He intended it to be.

Let's take a look at some specific chains that hold you captive to the fear of failure. Through Christ, you can break free from this bondage and unleash the burning passion that will get you moving forward in life.

FEAR OF FAILURE

QUESTION >>>

> WHO SAYS YOU ARE A FAILURE?

When you consider taking risks to follow your dreams or stepping out in faith to do what God has called you to do, what holds you back? Specifically, what are you afraid will happen? Have there been times in the past when you tried and failed?

If you feel like a failure, it is because there is a person or standard you don't think you can measure up to. Somewhere along the way, someone told you what it would take for you to be successful, but when you look at your life, it doesn't match what they said. Or maybe you've bought into society's measure for success. You look at the happy people in the movies and magazines and know your life is far from what they portray. Whatever it is that labels you a failure, you have probably lost hope of ever succeeding.

According to your parents, siblings, friends, boss or coworkers, what would it take for you to be successful? Think about it and try writing it down. Now, do you think their standard is the same as God's? Do you think God is interested in what you look like, how much money you make or how you stand out in a crowd?

To get out of this cycle of defeat, you first have to identify whose standard you are trying to measure up to. What do people say you have to be? You have to learn how to live above those demands. Man's expectations do not determine your success.

So I ask you, who says you are a failure?

FEAR OF FAILURE

TRUTH >>>

> A NEW REFERENCE FOR SUCCESS

The truth is, there is only one opinion that matters. Only One has the right to set a standard and expect you to keep it. Your father or mother, sister or brother, friend or coworker – their expectations are not important. Only God's standard matters.

God is the King of kings and Lord of lords. He is the Beginning and the End. He created you, and He saved you. What is man compared to Him? What can man do for you that God cannot?

Living up to God's standard may sound scary. It seems like His measure for success should be even higher than man's. He is perfect, so doesn't He want us to be perfect too? No way! God knows we are not perfect; He knows we falter and stumble.

That is why His reference for success is not about getting everything right. God doesn't see failure as falling down and making mistakes. Success to Him is rolled up in two things: faith and obedience.

It is God who has placed a calling on your life. He knows the potential that is burning to get out of you, and He designed it so you can only be successful in that calling when you trust and obey Him.

Any time you turn your eyes away from these goals, you will start to focus on man's reference for success. You may try and try to get it right, but you will never fully measure up. When you approach a new opportunity already feeling like a failure, you are more likely to run away in fear than pursue it.

This is where all of that starts to change. Once you set a new reference for success that matches God's, you don't have to be afraid of disappointing your friends and family any longer. Faith and obedience are within the grasp of every believer, including you, and that means success is also within your reach.

FEAR OF FAILURE

TESTIMONY >>>

I HEARD GOD SPEAK WITH MY WHOLE BEING

Running down a soccer field at age 23, I heard the voice of the Lord Jesus Christ for the first time. I didn't hear the voice with my ears . . . it was much louder than that. I heard God speak with my whole being. And when He spoke, I knew His voice as well as I knew my own mother's or father's.

He said to me, "Eddie, are you going to run after this ball for the rest of your life, or are you going to run after me like you are running after that ball?"

Right there, I responded to the voice of God. I made a decision to stop running after the ball and start running after souls. My goal no longer sits at the end of the soccer field. No, my goal is to see souls come to Christ and to see you set free from fear by the power of God. That is my mission.

FEAR OF
FAILURE

KEY

 **GOD SPEAKS**

Perhaps you are reading this, and you know there is something you were created to do, but you just can't quite figure out what that something is. I want to reassure you that God does have a specific plan for you. You just need to ask Him what it is.

But does God speak to us? How can we hear Him? When we ask Him questions, how do we know when He answers? And when we think He answers, how can we be sure He was the one speaking?

God does speak to His people, and there are some specific ways to know when He is speaking and when He is not. When I say that "God told me" or "God spoke to me," I want you to understand what I mean so that you can hear Him too.

Let me ask you, the last time you thought God was leading you or speaking to you, what emotions did you have? Were you at peace with what was in your soul? Or did questions and uncertainty linger in the back of your mind?

If you still fear failure, if questions drag you down, don't pursue it. Just continue to ask God for His direction and voice. Wait for the peace that passes all understanding so you can be secure and confident you have heard the word of the Lord.

God's voice – His Word, wisdom and direction – always come with peace. When He speaks, a stillness comes to your heart. You won't have to question whether it was God. You will know by the peace that accompanies the voice. And when you know it was God's voice that you heard, run with it!

KEY

FEAR OF FAILURE

ECHO >>>

MOVE FORWARD

Once God has revealed His purpose to you, you can <u>move forward</u>, blowing past that fear of failure to land in a place of great success. You can press forward to accomplish all that He has placed in your heart. Let me give you three keys that will unlock the door to success for your dreams.

The first two I have already mentioned – faith and obedience. Only God is perfect. His ways are perfect, and He is powerful enough to accomplish even the most impossible dreams. That is why faith in Him is necessary for success. Always remember, we can do all things *through Christ* who strengthens us (Philippians 4:13). It is *through Christ* that we have success. Unless we believe in Him to accomplish it, success will not come.

Second, we must be obedient. This step is a simple one: When God says to do something, do it! No matter if it makes sense to you, no matter if others agree with what you are doing, just do it. I love the psalm that describes the person who follows God's ways. It says he is like a "tree planted by the rivers of water, that brings forth its fruit in its season . . . and *whatever he does shall prosper*"(Psalm 1:3 NKJV).

The last key to true success is an exciting one. It only comes after you have trusted God and obeyed what He has told you to do. You see, whenever you are committed to knowing your Maker in these ways, you enter into a new dimension – a dimension of favor with God and man. With God's favor, no man can be against you, no matter what they say or think about you. God's favor will carry you through impossible situations that would otherwise cause you to fail.

When you trust God and walk in His ways, His favor falls upon you in such a way that success is inevitable. Listen to God's promise in Proverbs 3:1-4:

My son, do not forget my teaching, but keep my commands in your heart, for they will prolong your life many years and bring you prosperity. Let love and faithfulness never leave you; bind them around your neck, write them on the tablet of your heart. Then you will win favor and a good name in the sight of God and man.

You cannot accomplish anything special without both the favor of God and the favor of man. Obedience leads to favor. Favor with God and man means guaranteed success in whatever you attempt.

ECHO

FEAR OF FAILURE

SONG > > >

> HIGH ON LOVE

I wish that you could see me now
I'm driving in my beat-up car
Heading down to who knows where
The wind is blowing in my hair
I wish that you could feel this way
And feel the wind of sweet release
Money could never pay for such an awesome day

I never thought that I could feel this good again
But look at me, here I am, a brand-new man
And I don't want to run, I don't want to hide from this feeling
I'm willing to fight, I'm willing to try to reach higher
I wish that everyone of you could feel the way I do
So let the whole world know I'm high on love

I wish that you could see me now
I'm passing by a sandy beach
My T-top's down, the sun is hot
I'm loving every moment that I got
My heart is flowing with your love
I've been touched by heaven above
Your name is written in my heart
You've given me a brand-new start

I never thought that I could feel this good again
But look at me, here I am, a brand-new man
And I don't want to run, I don't want to hide from this feeling
I'm willing to fight, I'm willing to try to reach higher
I wish that everyone of you could feel the way I do
So let the whole world know I'm high on love

I wanna go a little deeper
I wanna fly a little higher
I'm not ashamed to let it show
So let the whole world know

And I don't want to run, I don't want to hide from this feeling
I'm willing to fight, I'm willing to try to reach higher
I wish that everyone of you could feel the way I do
So let the whole world know I'm high on love

FEAR OF
FAILURE

PRAYER > > >

> FATHER, APPLY YOUR PERFECT LOVE

Father, I come before you in the name of Jesus, thanking you that you are always with us. Thank you for surrounding my friends with Your favor that covers them like a shield. Thank you for taking all the things that come in their lives and working them for good.

I ask You, Lord, to give them the faith and obedience to put their hands to the plow, seeking to fulfill the dreams, visions and desires You have placed in them. And when they do, remove all fear of failure from them. Apply Your perfect love to their lives and cast out all fear from their hearts. Thank you, Lord, that as long as we obey You, we are secure in You. And thank You that even when we fall, Lord, you will pick us up.

We love You, Lord, and we trust You.
Amen

FEAR OF FAILURE

CHALLENGE >>>

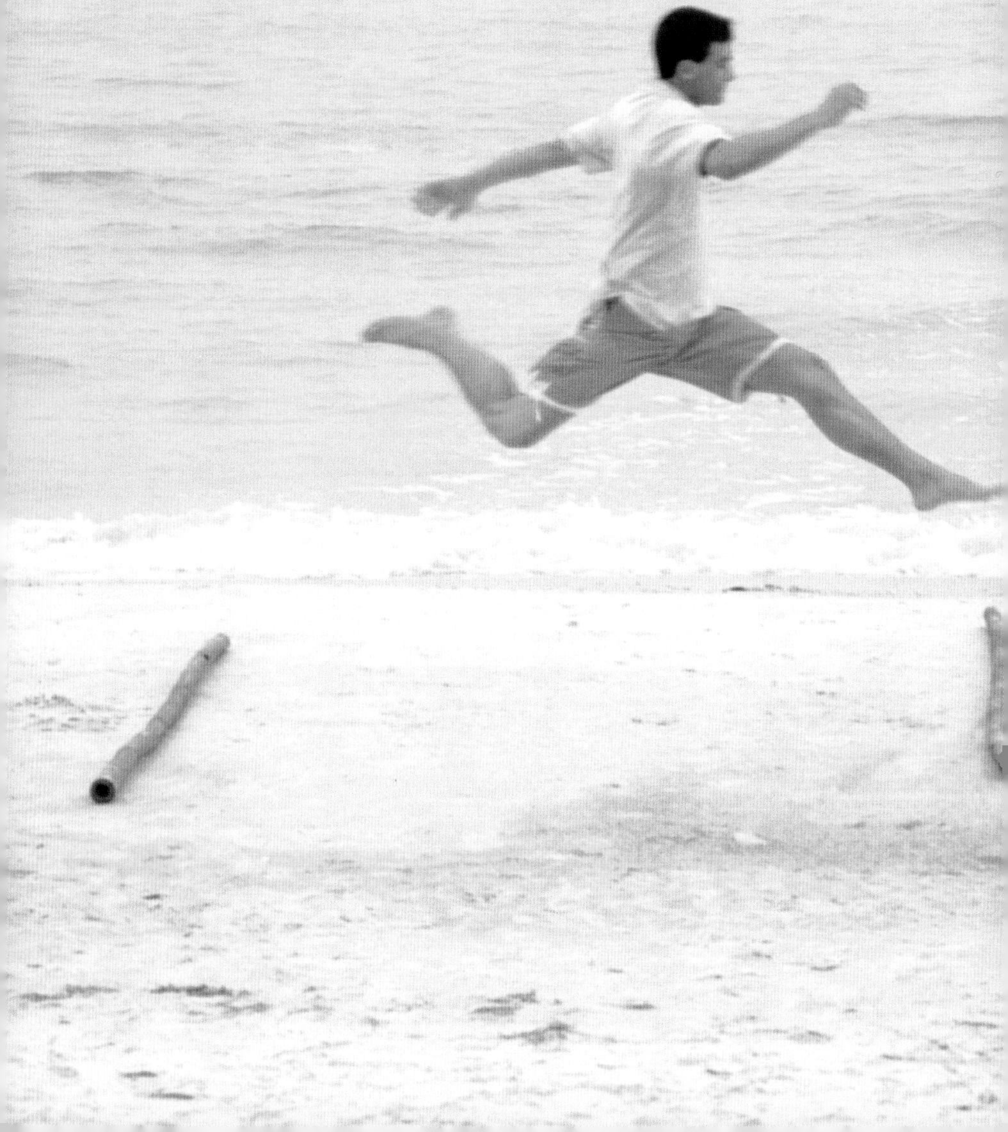

DON'T BE AFRAID

Friends, I know that you have tried many times and have given up. If someone has convinced you that your dreams are impossible, know they are wrong! Jesus said, "Everything is possible for him who believes" (Mark 9:23).

God is perfect, and God is love. The Bible says, "perfect love casts out fear" (1 John 4:18 NKJV). Get to know your Maker. Trust Him. Obey Him. Let His perfect love drive away the fear that is holding you back from pursuing your hopes and dreams.

Once you set your hand to the plow, don't look back again (Luke 9:62). Don't start listening to those voices again. Only listen to God's voice and press on! And know when you choose to serve God, the favor of the Lord will come upon you and you will never be the same again.

Don't be afraid to reach higher. Pursue all the vision God has given you. Don't be afraid to go deeper. Run with it! Success will come as you reach higher and wider. The victory is yours because God wants you to win. He wants you to prosper. He wants you to go from glory to glory, turning your entire life into an instrument of praise.

FEAR OF LONELINESS

FEAR OF LONELINESS

INTRO >>>

God has a plan for your life, but that plan will never come to pass if you let fear keep you from stepping out in faith and obedience. Fear holds you back from the purpose and destiny you were created for.

Most people are terrified of loneliness. The thought of being by ourselves scares us to death! Unfortunately, being alone is inevitable. All of us are by ourselves at some point in time. We can be surrounded by people and still feel very lonely.

However, Christians should never fear loneliness . . . they should embrace it! You see, our enemy has led us to believe that if we feel alone in the world, then we are alone in the world. But for a child of God, that is not true. God has said, "Never will I leave you; never will I forsake you" (Hebrews 13:5). And Jesus Himself told us, ". . . surely I am with you always, to the very end of the age" (Matthew 28:20).

There you have it – when you know Christ, when God is your Father, you are never alone. Even though you may feel abandoned, rejected or neglected, it is not true. God has accepted you, and He loves you. At every moment, He is with you.

There is no reason to fear loneliness. Some people go to any extreme to avoid being alone, but I challenge you to be different. Embrace loneliness! God has a purpose for the loneliness He allows in your life, a very exciting reason. Would you like to know what it is?

Stay with me here, keep reading, and I will show you what God has taught me about loneliness. When you discover His purpose behind it, you won't have to be afraid of it anymore.

FEAR OF LONELINESS

QUESTION >>>

WHY DO I FEEL SO ALONE?

Before we dive into the life-changing truth about loneliness, I want you to spend a moment in introspection. Think. When do you feel most lonely? What makes you feel that way?

The emotions that go along with loneliness can be intense and devastating: frustration, depression, despair and hopelessness. These feelings are what scare people. When someone longs for companionship, he or she will often stoop to desperate measures to escape the feelings of loneliness.

Are you in a lonely place now? Can you remember a particularly lonely time? Have you ever wanted to give up because it seemed like life would never get any better?

God has placed something unique inside of you. That something wants to be known. It wants to get outside of you and shine. But when no one seems to recognize you for who you really are, you feel alone. When your potential is ignored, you grow frustrated and even depressed.

Loneliness stems out of our frustration of not connecting with people. They don't understand us at our deeper levels, and we feel like no one on earth gets us. Either people abandon us or we abandon them, and then we find ourselves alone. As for that something inside of us that burns, we shut it off. And once we shut it off, we lose hope.

When hope is gone, when no one is there for you, when you can't seem to get out of bed, loneliness has taken you to its darkest point. But remember: God has a purpose. Loneliness doesn't have to end in depression and despair.

FEAR OF LONELINESS

TRUTH >>>

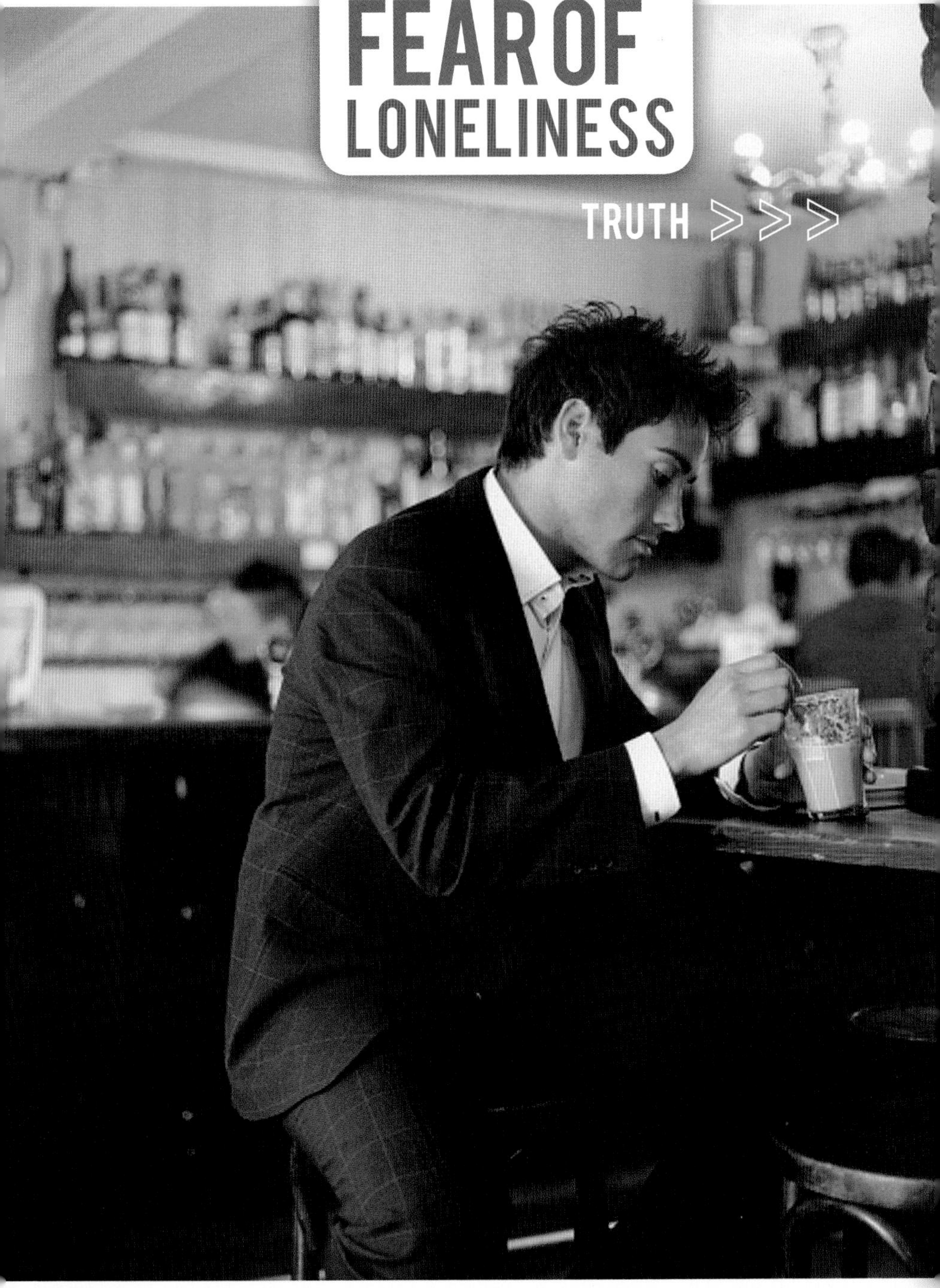

> THE PURPOSE OF LONELINESS

God loves you. He is your Father, and you are His child. Never does He allow things into your life, good or bad, unless they are for your good and His glory. Loneliness is no exception to this rule.

He has promised us that He will never leave us, and that means we are never actually alone. No matter how lonely we feel, the reality is that He is with us. So when loneliness attacks, we have to remember that God is already there. We don't have to call on Him or wait for Him; He is there. All we have to do is turn to Him and spend time with Him.

God allows you to get to a lonely state because He wants you to come to Him. He wants you to depend on Him and Him alone. When you have nobody and nothing except Him, you will start to learn just how sufficient He is for your every need and want.

When you do turn to Him, He turns the lonely times into training times. That something inside of you – that something that no one else seems to understand – God wants to refine it and bring it out of you. In the lonely times when you run to Him, He teaches you how to shine.

I call this "kingship training." God has placed a king inside of each one of us. That unique calling and passion is His investment of kingship inside of us. He wants you to live in that kingship just as much as you do. But before this can happen, He needs to train you and prepare you to live up to your kingship.

Imagine the difference it would make if we embraced our lonely times as anointed times, appointed by the Lord, to release the potential in our hearts. Instead of wallowing in depression or despair, if we ran to the Father and spent time with Him, He would transform us into the kings He intended us to be.

Friends, in the darkest, most alone seasons of your life, God wants to prepare you for greatness!

FEAR OF LONELINESS

TESTIMONY >>>

> I DIDN'T EVEN WANT TO WAKE UP

Depression and loneliness can get the best of me sometimes. When they do, my whole life feels black, like nothing will ever work out. A few years back, I was convinced that my life was meaningless. I knew God had placed something special inside of me, but I felt like it was stuck there.

All I wanted to do was sleep. I didn't want to wake up in the morning. I didn't want to face the day. Sometimes, I stayed in bed until four in the afternoon! After years of facing obstacles and wondering what my life was all about, I felt like I couldn't handle it anymore. I wondered what the point of living was. I wondered, *If life is going to be this difficult, why even face tomorrow?*

Then, in the middle of this dark season, crisis struck. My father died. My daddy, my best friend, my mentor and guide . . . I lost him. He had always been there to help me, and then, in a split second, he wasn't there anymore. I sunk even further into despair.

Never before and never since have I felt so depressed and alone. It took time, a lot of time, for God to get me through. But during that season of loneliness, He taught me something very important. Depression does not have to defeat. God allows it in my life so that I will seek Him.

He had placed something special inside of me, and He was trying to train me to use it. No one in my life could bring out my potential, only Jesus. Only He could make my dreams and visions come true. My dad couldn't get me there . . . only Jesus can. Depression and loneliness made me turn to God, and I have found that when I earnestly, diligently, passionately seek Him, He trains me to be everything He created me to be.

I've been lonely so many times. But God sees my tears; He knows every time I am down or frustrated. And because I know how He wants to use those difficult times, I turn to Him. God has shown me that it is not about depression or frustration, but it is all about Him. Our first and utmost purpose in life is to know God and fellowship with Him. So when He draws us to Himself, whether through loneliness or whatever, we are fulfilling our purpose. When we spend time with Him, we are living our destiny.

FEAR OF LONELINESS

KEY > > >

> LONELINESS — YOUR BEST FRIEND

Loneliness is not the enemy. It is our friend! Anything that drives us to God is our friend. In fact, if we embrace it for all God intended it for, it can be our best friend! Only God can take the negative emotions of life's dark times and turn them into kingship training.

Let me challenge you today. When you start to feel lonely, don't get frustrated or depressed. Don't get angry or desperate. Instead, right away, draw near to God. The Bible says that when we draw near to God, He will draw near to us (James 4:8). Get on your knees. Cry out to Him in honesty. Open the Bible and let God speak His love and truth over you.

You will be surprised how different your life is when you embrace loneliness. The adversary loses his grip on you when you refuse to buy his lies that you are alone. And when you let God use the lonely times to transform you, you will come out of that season a king.

Learn from the lives of Joseph, Moses and David. Just when life hits rock bottom, just when it appears that you are alone in the world without hope of tomorrow ever getting better, know that God is working. He is drawing you to Himself. He is calling you to greatness . . . to your kingship!

Once you have shaken off the fear of loneliness, start to follow Jesus' example. Even when you don't feel lonely, seek out alone times with God. Get away from the noise and busyness of life. Seek refuge in His presence and let Him change you.

FEAR OF LONELINESS

ECHO >>>

SNAPSHOTS OF LONELINESS

THE DREAMER

From childhood, Joseph was known as a dreamer. When he was young, he dreamed of becoming a great leader, even ruling over his family. You can imagine, these dreams did not impress his older brothers. After a while, they became so annoyed with his dreams that they sold him into slavery.

Away from his loving parents, his family, friends and home, Joseph spent the next many years completely alone. Serving with diligence and integrity as a slave in the house of a wealthy Egyptian, he became known for his hard, honest work. Joseph rose within the household to manage everything for his master.

Life was looking up, but then his master's wife tried to seduce him. When he refused her, she turned the tables on him and accused him of rape. His master sent him straight to prison. Again stripped of anything familiar, everyone kind, the work he enjoyed and excelled at, Joseph was alone. Only this time, he was alone in prison.

Through a miraculous series of events, the Pharaoh came to know of Joseph and his God-given ability to interpret dreams. After Joseph accurately interpreted the Pharaoh's dream about an oncoming famine, the Pharaoh promoted him to second in command over all Egypt. He was in charge of managing the food supply so that those in need during the famine would not starve.

After years of being separated from family, not recognized as anything more than a slave or prisoner, God exalted Joseph to his kingship. God used those years of loneliness to prepare him for the time when he would rise to leadership and save the lives of countless people, including his family.

ECHO

FEAR OF LONELINESS

ECHO >>>

SNAPSHOTS OF LONELINESS

THE SOJOURNER

Moses must have been confused about family and loyalty. He was born in a Hebrew slave family, but raised by the Pharaoh's daughter. When he grew up and tried to take justice into his own hands, killing an Egyptian man who was beating a Hebrew, he was forced to flee his homeland.

Moses ran for his life, leaving everything familiar behind – his Hebrew-birth family and his Egyptian-adopted family. Escaping to the east, he traveled the vast desert all alone before he found civilization once again.

When he finally arrived in the land of Midian, Moses met Jethro, a priest and his seven daughters. Moses took one of the daughters to be his wife and settled among them, but life was nothing like it had been in Egypt. Instead of living with royal privileges, Moses herded his father-in-law's flocks.

For forty years, Moses lived away from his homeland among strangers and a strange culture. The days must have seemed endless with only livestock for company.

Moses didn't know that God was using those dull days and quiet nights to prepare him for something great. Speaking from a burning bush, God called Moses out of his loneliness to step into the kingship He had been training him for. You know the story. Moses stood up to Egypt, the most powerful nation in the world, led his people out of slavery, through the Red Sea and all the way to the borders of God's Promised Land.

ECHO

FEAR OF LONELINESS

ECHO >>>

> SNAPSHOTS OF LONELINESS

THE REFUGEE

David was the youngest, and perhaps least noteworthy, of eight brothers. However, when the prophet Samuel came looking for the man God had chosen to be the next king, he recognized David right away. God had placed a great calling of leadership on David. Right there, in front of David's family, Samuel anointed him as king.

Still very young, David would not assume his throne for many, many years. In fact, after Samuel left him, he went back to tending his father's sheep. Later, when King Saul saw God's power and anointing on David's life, he chased David around the wilderness trying to kill him.

This was a dark time for David; he felt abandoned by everyone, including God. God had promised to make David king; He had given David His Spirit of power. But there David was, forced to run for his life, seeking refuge in caves.

After many close calls, battles, scandals and heartbreaks, David finally became King of Israel. Undoubtedly, God used those lonely nights in the fields and caves to prepare him for the immense job of leading His chosen people.

FEAR OF LONELINESS

ECHO >>>

SNAPSHOTS OF LONELINESS

THE LONER

Jesus was no stranger to loneliness. If there was ever a misunderstood, underestimated man, it was Jesus. Within Him, He held the glory and majesty of God, but to his neighbors, He was just a carpenter. To many of His followers, He was just a good teacher. Even His disciples mistook Him, thinking He would be an earthly, militant king sent by God to overthrow the Romans.

Until He rose from the grave, no one really got Jesus. He must have spent many lonely moments, surrounded by crowds of people who wanted Him to be someone else, someone less than He was. Of course, the loneliest time for Jesus was when he hung on the cross. The masses had condemned Him. His friends had betrayed Him. God had turned away from Him. With the sins of the world weighing on His shoulders, Jesus bore them completely alone.

What is remarkable about Jesus' journey is that loneliness didn't find Jesus. Jesus sought it out. He did not fear it, but ran to it and embraced it. The Bible tells us that early in the morning, Jesus would go to solitary places to pray (Mark 1:35). After serving and teaching the crowds, He went to a mountainside alone to talk with His Father (Matthew 14:23). Even the night before He was crucified, Jesus went off by Himself to pray (Luke 22:41).

Jesus is the King of kings. He is the Son of God. He was the perfect man. Never once did He run from loneliness or try to escape the feelings. Never did He shrink back from His Kingship. Instead, He found strength in God's presence. He rose to His position of Kingship, and He let God lead Him there through times of loneliness.

ECHO

FEAR OF LONELINESS

SONG >>>

NOT ALONE

It's not the first time I find myself sitting alone
I'm close to home, downtown, at the local café
I'm looking around, but I'm not there, no
I'm somewhere far away, I'm long gone
In my own world, miles and miles from here
And in my world I can see you smiling back at me
I can feel you holding me so tenderly

Truth is, I'm not alone
Sitting in a corner by myself
Truth is, I'm not alone
Wishing I could be somebody else
Truth is

I'm not surprised to find out
That what would become after all this time is a beautiful thing,
Just you and I, I can't get you out of my mind
Now you're in me and I'm in You
What better way to make my dream come true
Than to fall in love heart and soul and live forevermore
And in my world I can see you smiling back at me
I can feel you holding me so tenderly

Truth is, I'm not alone
Sitting in a corner by myself
Truth is, I'm not alone
Wishing I could be somebody else
Truth is

Where could I hide from the love that you bring me
What would I be if you were not with me?
Why would I let go of something so special when . . .

Truth is, I'm not alone
Sitting in a corner by myself
Truth is, I'm not alone
Wishing I could be somebody else
Truth is

FEAR OF
LONELINESS

PRAYER >>>

> FATHER, OPEN THEIR EYES

Father in heaven, thank you for seeing everything we go through.
You see our hearts and minds, and You always know how we feel.
Thank You for loving us and for planting kingship in our hearts.

Right now, I come to You on behalf of my friends who are battling
loneliness. Be their comfort and be their truth. Open their eyes,
Father, to see the reality of their loneliness. Give them the strength
and faith to turn to You. Help them run to You. And when they do,
Lord, be their ever-present help in trouble. Meet the longing in their
hearts for love, companionship and greater purpose.

Lord, work a miracle in their lives like you did for Joseph, Moses and
David. Use the hard times they struggle through as kingship training.
You have placed passion and calling on their lives, and now they need
to be trained to accomplish them. Step into their seasons of loneliness
and transform them into seasons of preparation.

Father, erase the fear of loneliness and replace it with confidence in
You. Give my friends the faith to embrace lonely times, knowing that
You are bringing the king out in them.

PRAYER

FEAR OF
LONELINESS

CHALLENGE >> >> >>

CONQUER LONELINESS

Now you know – loneliness is a gift from God. He draws you to Himself through loneliness to prepare you for kingship. Now you can defeat the loneliness that has haunted you for so long. You can beat it by embracing its purpose.

When you find yourself in the valley of decision, grappling with frustration, hopelessness, depression or despair, call on Jesus! He told us that He is the way we are looking for (John 14:6). When He placed those dreams, visions, desires and passions in your heart, He also made a way to see them come to pass. Allow loneliness to be His tool for releasing you to live in the success and joy of your calling.

Remember, loneliness in not a bad thing. It is your path to kingship.

CHALLENGE

FEAR OF
MAN

FEAR OF MAN

MAN

INTRO ≫ ≫ ≫

THE ENEMY'S TOOL

The enemy wants to steal your destiny. His plan is to bring you low and take away any hope of reaching your dreams. If you don't know who you are and where you are from, you will fall for his snare.

God, on the other hand, wants to help you achieve your destiny. Fear holds us back from that, which is why God did not give us a spirit of fear, but of power, love and self-discipline (2 Timothy 1:7). Your Father is the only one who can drive you to your ordained destiny, so you should trust and follow Him above all else.

So far, we have tackled two fears that keep us from living in God's freedom: failure and loneliness. In the case of these two, we are afraid of emotions and feelings. Now I want to talk to you about the fear of something much more tangible and real: the fear of man.

The enemy uses the fear of man to hold you back. If you can beat this fear factor, you will find incredible freedom. My mom used to tell me that while people can strip everything from you, they can never take your dream. Your dreams are the driving force behind your purpose. If man manages to steal your dreams, it is because you have fallen for the adversary's snare and he has used the fear of man to beat you.

Look with me at this tool of the enemy that traps so many of us and causes us to lose sight of our vision and dreams.

INTRO

FEAR OF
MAN

QUESTION >>>

> WHOSE OPINION MATTERS?

When we talked about the fear of failure, I asked you who determines success and failure in your life – God or your parents, spouse, siblings, friends or coworkers. Now I'm going even deeper and asking you, what do people think of you? Not just as a failure or success, but what do they think of you as a parent, friend, Christian, etc.

Everyone has an opinion about what others should be or do . . . and everyone's opinion is different. If you try to please them all, you will go crazy! One person thinks you should do one thing while another thinks you should do something completely different. It is impossible to get it right in everyone's eyes.

Whose opinion matters to you most? If you could only please one person, who would that be? When you center your life around pleasing anyone, you will feel only as worthy as they deem you.

Whom do you trust to place expectations on you that are achievable and true to your calling? Whose opinion of you is always based on love and acceptance?

QUESTION

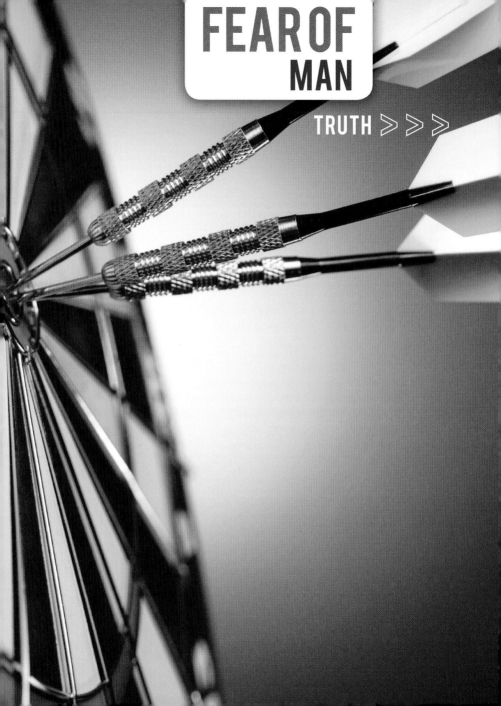

FEAR OF MAN

TRUTH >>>

SAFE IN CHRIST

No one is perfect. None of us have it completely together. Most of us get weary trying to be good enough, smart enough or strong enough. And if "enough" is set by man (a spouse, parent, sibling or friend), we will always come up short.

That is why the only opinion that matters is God's. He sent Jesus, and in Christ our "enough" was met on the cross. Jesus completely defended us when He died, and therefore we are completely accepted by the Father. Nothing we do or don't do could ever make us "not enough" in God's eyes.

It is no secret that we have made mistakes, a lot of mistakes. If we had to carry the weight of all those mistakes for the rest of our lives, it would be impossible to press on to achieve our dreams. But Jesus took the blame for our mistakes. He paid our debt with His blood. He was found guilty for our sins. When we receive His forgiveness, we can shed the burden of those past mistakes and carry on with joy and strength.

You are very special to your creator. He wants to have the only opinion that matters to you. When you turn to man to find significance or purpose, you will only discover frustration and impossibilities. But when you turn to your Father as your reference point, you will discover unparalleled peace and security.

TRUTH

FEAR OF MAN

TESTIMONY ≫ ≫ ≫

When I was still young in ministry, a pastor from Oklahoma, Pastor Bussett, asked me to come sing at his church. This was my first opportunity to minister to a church in that way, and I was so nervous. When I arrived, I was literally sweating with fear because I didn't think I could do it. I was afraid of how people would perceive me as an artist because I didn't feel like I had what it took to deliver a message from God.

Despite my feelings, something in me said, "I gotta do this." So I pressed on. At the church, the pastor introduced me as a young Norwegian singer who would bring brilliant songs. After that, I walked up on stage and the pastor sat down. There I stood: alone, nervous and intimidated. And then it happened. I forgot all of my songs. I couldn't remember the words, the tunes or even how to place my fingers on the guitar. So overwhelmed with fear, I began to cry. Can you imagine? In front of all those people, all I could do was weep!

I stood there confounded and confused, but something inside of me said again, "Eddie, press on." So I grabbed my guitar and told

the congregation, "Guys, I'm gonna sing you a song." I didn't
know what to call it, so I made up a name. Then I just began to play.
Miraculously, out of my spirit came a verse, a chorus, another verse,
a chorus, a bridge and another chorus – a perfect song. Today, I
can't even remember how that song went.

Then I turned to the audience and started crying again because I
felt so out of control. Out of my frustration, I told them I would sing
another song. And again, a verse, a chorus, a verse, a chorus, a
bridge and a chorus – another perfect song was laid before
the people.

When I stepped off that stage, I felt like the biggest failure in the
whole world. I felt stupid, like I couldn't deliver what I was supposed
to deliver.

I left the church after the service that morning and went home
embarrassed, convinced I would never sing in church again. After
a miserable afternoon of feeling like a failure, the phone rang at
around 6 pm. It was Pastor Bussett. He said, "Edward John, you
don't know what you've done to my church."

"I am so sorry, Pastor," I apologized. "I should never have sung
at your church. I didn't know what I was doing. I stepped out
too early."

"No, Edward," he replied. "You don't understand what's happened,"
he explained. "From 11:00 this morning until 6:00 this evening,
the people in the church have been weeping under the presence
of God."

I learned in that moment, it is not about how good I am or what I
know. It is not about how much ability I have. It is about how much
I dare to lose control, taking focus off myself to let God work
through me.

FEAR OF
MAN

KEY >>>

Fear of man has a simple solution: Shift your focus from man to God. Shift authority from man's word to God's Word.

To be intimidated means you have to spend a lot of time and energy focusing on one person or group of people. They have become your standard, your hope and your obsession. You have to shift that focus to God. Jesus has already met the standard for you, so placing your hope in Him will only bring you success!

If a compliment from someone important in your life can make your day, their criticism can definitely ruin it. That is because you have made their words an authority in your life. Whatever they say, you believe to be true. Only God's Word should hold that place in your life. No man can substitute what God has said. The Bible is the measure and standard by which we are to live; it tells us who we are or who we are supposed to be.

The fear of man continues to grip you in defeat because you are focused on the wrong things: man's opinion and man's words. Shifting those to God will set you free to finally live with joy and motivation to run to the finish line with confidence.

FEAR OF
MAN

ECHO >>>

Refusing to fear man means honoring God and His Word above all else. Turn your focus to the verses listed here and learn more about what it looks like to fully trust God with your dreams and your future.

Whoever finds his life will lose it, and whoever loses his life for my sake will find it. Matthew 10:39

The only way to break the fear of man from your life is by making a solid choice to lay your life down. Instead of trusting yourself to accomplish your destiny, you have to trust God. Your entire life focus must be geared toward loving and serving Him. If you are used to staying in complete control of your life, this may be hard. But it is worth it. How much do you dare to lose control?

Trust in the LORD with all your heart and lean not on your own understanding; in all your ways acknowledge him, and he will make your paths straight. Proverbs 3:5-6

Trusting God with every decision, every step and every feeling is the only way to pursue your dream with success. He is the only one who can build the bridge to your destiny. He knows the way, so trust and follow Him.

"The righteous will live by faith." Romans 1:17

And without faith it is impossible to please God . . . Hebrews 11:6

People say you can't live by faith, but God says you must. We were created to know God, and we know Him through faith. Faith pleases God, and making Him happy should be our highest goal.

Therefore, if anyone is in Christ, he is a new creation; the old has gone, the new has come! 2 Corinthians 5:17

Make the decision today to get rid of self, and instead, clothe yourself with Christ. Your faith in Him, trust in Him and abandonment to Him will conform you into a new creation, free from the fear of man.

ECHO

> DON'T BE SWAYED BY MAN

Jesus is always our ultimate example. He lived perfectly so that when we follow Him, we walk a path of fearless living straight into our destiny. If you look at Jesus' life, you will notice that He was never swayed by man.

Jesus came as the long awaited Messiah, but the way He came, the things He did and the words He spoke were not accepted by people. Pharisees told Him constantly not to do certain things. His followers questioned His teachings. No one seemed to understand why He had to die.

But Jesus, the Son of God, was on a mission. He had a calling and a purpose that He would not waver from. Nothing man could say or do would deter Him from His path.

One of my songs, "Find Me Guilty," tells about the highest calling of love, which is to die for others. That is what Jesus did for us. He took our blame and our place on the cross so that we can carry on. He pled guilty for the sake of love. He laid down His life for us when it mattered most. Even when life was hardest for Him, when His friends deserted Him, when the crowds yelled to crucify Him and the soldiers beat Him, He never gave in.

Jesus never let man sway Him, and with Him as our defender and strength, we don't have to either.

FEAR OF MAN

SONG > > >

FIND ME GUILTY

I will plead guilty if that's what you want
I don't mind going down for love
I play the game, for me it's the same
It don't matter to me anyway
Cause I would lay my life down for you
When everything is on the line
You can carry on if all the blame is mine

So find me guilty of reaching too high
I'm still aiming for the sky
For no greater love could no man find
Than for another be willing to die

I learn the hard way not to give in
It don't matter if I don't win
But I will defend you with all that I am
I'll take all the blows if I can
Cause I would lay my life down for you
When everything is on the line
You can carry on if all the blame is mine

So find me guilty of reaching too high
I'm still aiming for the sky
For no greater love could no man find
Than for another be willing to die

I'm just a man fighting for love
Looking for truth, living in hope
I'm just a man fighting for love
Looking for truth, living in hope

So find me guilty of reaching too high
I'm still aiming for the sky
For no greater love could no man find
Than for another be willing to die

FEAR OF
MAN

PRAYER >>>

 # LORD, SET US FREE

God in heaven, You created man in your image. You have loved us and even died to reconcile us back to you. Help us, Father, not to fear man or honor man more than we honor you. Thank you for giving us dear relationships with people whom we love. Thank you for meeting our needs through those relationships, but Lord, please help us not to run to man for help. Draw us to you.

I pray for my friends who struggle under the bondage of the fear of man. Set them free from the expectations, demands and words they are constantly trying to live up to. Give us all confidence in Your Son, Jesus, who died to defend us.

Lord, you know our hearts, how we want to move forward in life, free from the fear of man. Work in us. Set our trust, expectation and hope in You and You alone.

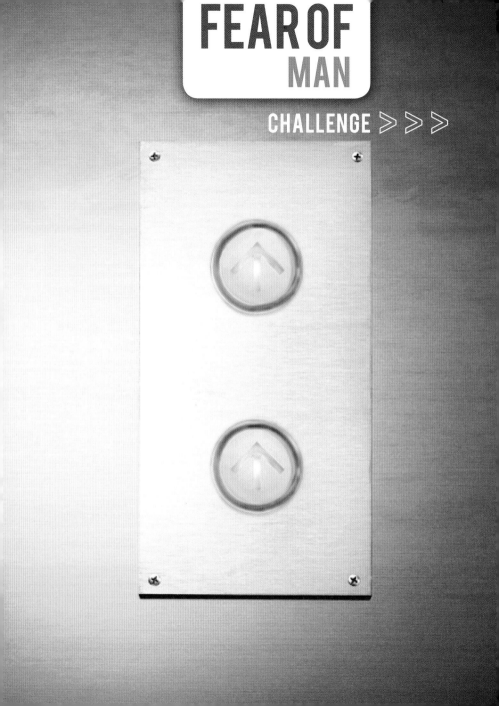

> CHOOSE AND LIVE

God has blessed every one of us with wonderful relationships. We have parents, husbands, wives, children and friends. And beyond these close relationships, we come in contact with countless others every day: bosses, coworkers and neighbors. People are all around us, and how we view and treat them is important.

Our fear of man usually stems from putting too much importance on them. Don't get me wrong; I strongly believe that we should love all mankind. The Bible commands us over and over to love one another (John 13:34), those less fortunate than us (Zechariah 7:9-10) and our families (Ephesians 5:22-6:4). Even for those we never meet or interact with, we should still have tremendous respect for them. Every person created carries the image of God and thus deserves our respect.

However, there is one thing we should reserve only for God – our honor. Never should we honor man before we honor God! Anyone we revere, we will fear. If we revere a certain sports figure, we will want to be like him or her. If we revere our mother, her opinion will matter more to us than anyone else's. If we revere friends, we will go to extreme lengths to please them.

In the same way, those we honor, we fear losing. We try so hard to do what others want us to do because we don't want them to abandon us. Even their disapproval feels like we've lost connection with them.

Honor should be reserved only for God. Only He gives us grace to be who we are because He created us to be that way. Only He gives us forgiveness when we mess up. Only He gives us strength to accomplish all that is in our hearts. Only He will never leave us or forsake us (Deuteronomy 31:6). Only He deserves our utmost praise and reverence.

Respect man. Love man. But above all, honor God.

FEAR OF GOD

FEAR OF GOD

GOD

INTRO >>>

> FEAR THAT STEALS JOY

"This is the day the Lord has made; let us rejoice and be glad in it" (Psalm 118:24). God has done so much for us so that we can be glad. He wants us to overflow with joy, to be full of vision, purpose and destiny. We do not serve a grumpy God who can't stand to see us having a good time, but a loving Father who delights in our joy and happiness.

The sad thing is, many Christians miss out on that joy. They just don't understand the true nature of God. Years of disappointments, misunderstandings and unfulfilled expectations have led them to believe that God is not interested in their purpose or happiness. Instead of running to God and embracing all He has for them, they run away from God in fear.

Being afraid of God is a sure way to rob yourself of life fulfillment and destiny. I've mentioned several times already that God is the one who created you with purpose and gifted you with vision. Only in Him can you accomplish all that He put in your heart. If you spend all your time trying to escape His presence though, there is no way you can connect with Him to truly reach your destiny.

Unlike your fears of failure, loneliness and man, you don't have to get rid of your fear of God. There is an unhealthy way to fear Him and a healthy way to fear Him. When you learn the proper way to view and respond to God, your entire life and future will radically change. Instead of cowering in God's presence and missing out on His blessings for you, you will revel in His shadow, receiving all the goodness your loving Father wants to bestow on you.

FEAR OF GOD

QUESTION >>>

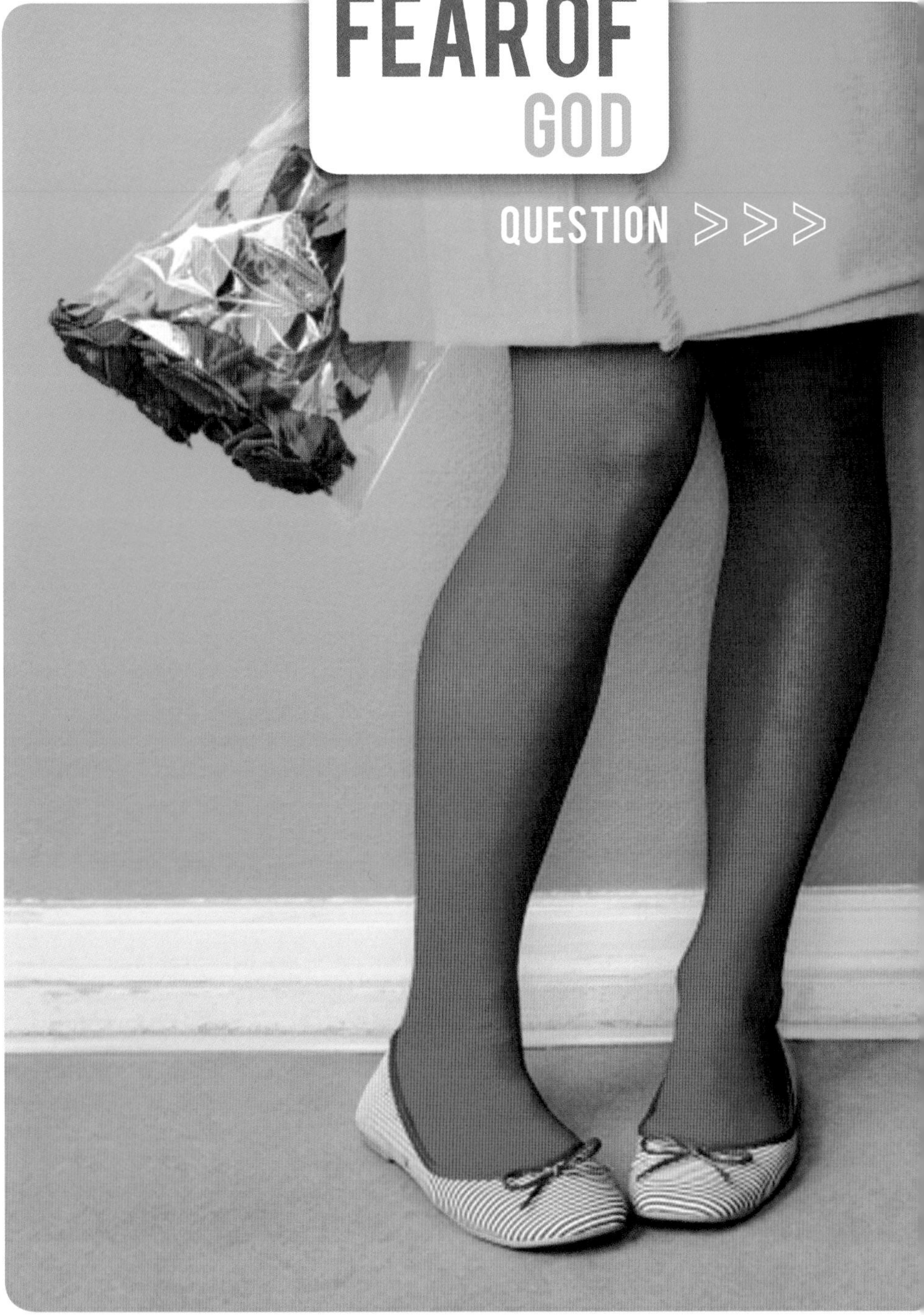

> HOW COULD GOD EVER LOVE ME?

Have you ever felt intimidated by God? When you read about His holiness and perfection, do you feel small and unworthy?

People who are afraid of God are usually insecure. Quite simply, they just don't feel worthy of God's love and acceptance. When they think back to past mistakes and sins, they start to think, How could God ever love me after all of that?

In James 4:8, God commands us, "Draw near to God and He will draw near to you" (NKJV). But with all the baggage we carry around, sometimes it feels wrong to draw near to God. Why would He want us anywhere near Him?

According to this verse, if we refuse to draw near to God, then we shouldn't expect Him to draw near to us. Think about this: When you sin, is it right or wrong to draw near to God? Is it right or wrong to run away from God when you have sinned? According to James 4:8, and remember that the Bible is the standard we base our lives on, it is wrong to run from God. That means it is always right to draw near to Him! Even though it feels wrong to approach a holy God when we have disobeyed or messed up, it's not.

God created you for pleasure, the pleasure of fellowship with Him. When we allow our sins and fears to keep us from Him, we miss out on fellowship with Him. That is how we miss out on our purpose, because God molds us and guides us to fulfill our destiny when we dwell in His presence.

When those guilt-ridden questions of self-worth come up, remember James 4:8. Choose to draw near to God no matter where you are coming from or what you have done.

FEAR OF
GOD

TRUTH >>>

> THE SHADOW OF THE ALMIGHTY

One of my favorite verses is Psalm 91:1: "He who dwells in the shelter of the Most High will rest in the shadow of the Almighty." There is something about dwelling in the shadow of God's presence . . . I find security and rest there like no other place on earth. Even when I come to Him carrying mistakes and troubles, I find the shadow of the Almighty welcoming and freeing.

God is a loving and perfect Father. He wants His children to be comfortable enough in His love that we run to Him no matter what. When we are weak, He wants us to run to Him. When we are brokenhearted, He wants us to run to Him. When we are burdened with problems, He wants us to run to Him. When we sin, He wants us to run to Him. His love is always enough.

If we run away instead, things will only get worse. Only in the shadow of the Almighty will we find what we need. Our destiny is fulfilled in God's presence. Our hearts are mended in God's presence. Our sins are forgiven in God's presence. You and I were created to live every day, every moment in God's presence.

God has called us first to Himself, to live in a close, intimate relationship. When we let the enemy scare us away from the goodness of God, we squander the calling and vision He has placed on our hearts. But when we fellowship with Him, we accomplish all of our life's purposes.

TRUTH

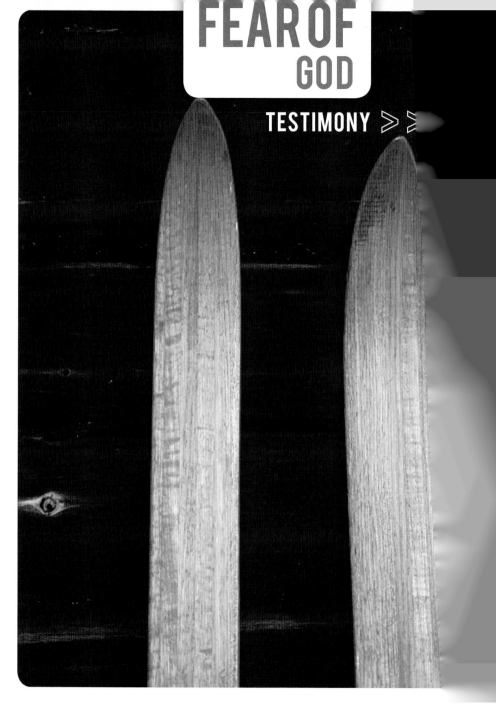

FEAR OF GOD

TESTIMONY >>

> DRAWING NEAR IN EVERY SITUATION

From the age of seven, I was a ski jumper in my home country of
Norway. When I was small, ski jumping wasn't really very scary.
But by the time I hit age twelve or thirteen, I started taking on
Olympic-size ski jumps. No matter how good I got at the sport,
those jumps were scary!

Before I would leave the house for the slopes, helmet under my
arm, skis on my shoulders and boots in my bag, my mom would
say to me, "Eddie, every time you do a jump, remember to say
'Dear Lord Jesus, be with me.' " I remember it like it was yesterday.

So every time I sat on that beam, looking down the slope I was
about to fly down at 65 miles an hour, and I got scared, I would
whisper that prayer under my breath: "Dear Lord Jesus, be with
me." Every time I prayed that, the fear disappeared and I got
through. In fact, I became one of the top ski jumpers for my nation
in my age group as a junior. I believe it was that prayer that made
me overcome the fear factors to become a good ski jumper.

Whatever you are facing in life – business, marriage, sports,
whatever – if you will simply pray a prayer like I did, God will
meet you where you are. Whenever you draw near to God, He
draws near to you.

TESTIMONY

FEAR OF GOD

KEY >>>

> FREEDOM RULES

One of the most intimidating things about God is His list of rules. If you've read the Bible, you've probably run across a few of them. Again, looking back at our track records, I'm sure none of us feel confident that we can live up to every one of them.

Maybe that is why you are afraid of God: You have tried and tried to be good enough according to the standard of His rules, and you keep falling short. It has become easier to run away from God and His expectations than to try to keep them all.

There are two things you need to understand about God's rules though. First is their purpose. When God says, "Don't lie, steal or hate," He does not do so to make life impossible or boring. You see, God is not like man. Often times, fathers are strict and harsh toward their children, driving them to rebellion, but God is no such Father.

The reason God gives us do's and dont's is to help us reach our potentials faster. He is the one who created us with purpose, and He knows the quickest path for us to accomplish those purposes. As our loving heavenly Father, He desires to help us move forward in life. He knows that sin keeps us from living our destinies and that walking in His ways puts us on the fast track to living out all that is in our hearts.

But just understanding why God has given us rules does not make these rules easier to keep. Nobody is perfect, and no one is exempt from sin. We have all sinned and fallen short of the glory of God. Even as Christians, we still have those old habits and ways tempting us, pulling us down. That is why we also need to understand that God gave us rules with only one way to keep them – with His power.

It is impossible to live a good life apart from Jesus. If we could do that, we wouldn't need God. But God wants us to need Him. He created us to depend on Him for everything. Living in His presence, asking Him for help and then obeying Him is the only way we can please Him and the only way we can ever hope to reach our dreams.

God's rules are not meant to restrict. He designed and commanded them so that they could help set us free from life patterns that hold us back, so that we can fully live out our destinies in Christ.

KEY

FEAR OF GOD

GOD

ECHO >>>

WHY FEAR GOD

God's nature, His rules, His ways – there is no reason to be afraid of any of these! I hope you see that now. But I would not be true to God's Word if I did not bring up what it says about fearing God.

Over and over, from Genesis to Revelation, the Bible tells us to "fear God." After all I have just told you about not being afraid of God, what do you think this could possibly mean? God is our loving Father who bestows goodness and blessing on us, so why fear Him?

The word "fear" has different meanings. So far, as we have talked about fearless living, we have used fear in the sense of being anxious or frightened. The thought of failure or loneliness stresses us out, and thus we fear or dread it. As we have already talked about, when we don't have a proper view of God, He can seem scary, and many people are frightened by Him.

But the word "fear" can also mean to revere or respect. The Bible tells us to fear God, not in the run-away-scared sense, but in the worship sense. We should stand in awe of who He is. While He is our Father and Friend, God is also the Creator of the universe, mighty and awe-inspiring. We are to praise His glory and never take for granted His power and might.

So, not to confuse you, but now that you know not to run from God, I encourage you to fear Him. Fall on your face before Him and worship Him. Do exactly what the Bible commands: "Fear God and keep his commandments" (Ecclesiastes 12:13).

ECHO

FEAR OF
GOD

ECHO >>>

> HEALTHY FEAR

King David provides a wonderful example of fearing God in a healthy way. The Bible tells us that David was a man after God's heart (Acts 13:22). This does not mean that David was perfect. No, he sinned even to the point of adultery and murder. However, David never ran away from God. Even after making so many mistakes, he had a heart that drew close to God. David knew that no matter what he did, he could always come back to his Father.

That is a healthy fear of God – one that knows and trusts the character of God completely. Without a healthy fear of God, you will be kept out of His love and protection. Without a healthy fear of God, you will miss out on His grace, forgiveness and help.

Every time you run away from God or try to hide from His presence, you run further and further away from His plan for your life. The desires of your heart, the passion that longs to break free can only be loosed through a relationship with God. Don't let fear hold you back! Run to Him. Receive His forgiveness, love and strength to sprint toward your destiny.

As you spend time in the presence of God, you will begin to grow in worship, one of the best ways to fear God in a healthy way. King David is among the greatest, most sincere worshippers who ever lived. He wrote dozens of psalms that are recorded in the Bible, songs that lift up the name and character of God.

David knew that worship connects God's children with their Father's heart. Every day I love to pour out my heart to Him. He loves it when I sing love songs to Him and tell Him how much I adore Him. And when I do, it opens the door for Him to work in my life.

My favorite song that I sing is simply called, "I Worship You." I have included the lyrics here because it will give you a glimpse of what it looks like for me to worship God. I hope it will inspire you to get in God's presence and fear Him through praise. I pray these words minister to you.

ECHO

FEAR OF
GOD

SONG >>>

I WORSHIP YOU

My door is closed my eyes
are shut
I'm on my knees and my hands
are up
Tears running down my face
I turn to you

My heart is weak I can
hardly speak
All my strength is gone
I'm all alone
I open up my heart to you
and worship you

Chorus

And I would give my last breath
for you
I would do anything you asked
me to
And I would give my life for you
That's why my door is closed
My eyes are shut
I'm on my knees
And my hands are up
And I worship you

Time seems gone
I'm holding on
Knowing that you will see
me through

And all your promises will
be fulfilled in me

All I do is believe in you
I trust in you
And know that it's true
And all that I have hoped for
It will come true

Chorus

That's what I love to do, just
worship you
I love every moment, of you
here by my side
That's why I'm on my knees,
seeking your face

Chorus

I worship you
Cause that's what I love
to do
I worship you
Cause that's what I'm born
to do

I worship you
Lord, for all you do
I worship you
Cause I simply love you

FEAR OF GOD

PRAYER >>>

> LORD, DRAW US NEAR

Father, right now we run to you. From wherever we have been hiding, we turn to You. We come with our sins, with our heartaches, with our problems and with our pain. We run to you because we know that You are a loving Father who waits to give us Your mercy and goodness.

Lord, draw us near to Your presence. We know that in Your presence is joy, and only when we come to You can we walk on the path of life. When we are afraid of You, God, please take that fear away. Remove it with Your steadfast love. Teach us how to fear You with reverence and praise. Teach us how to run to You every minute of every day.

We love You, Father. Make us fearless so that we can live out the destiny You have placed in our hearts. Bring glory to Yourself through our lives.

RUN TO YOUR FRIEND

Jesus told us that we are His friends (John 15:15). And just like we share everything with our earthly friends, we should do so with Jesus, too. Don't be afraid to go to Him with your ups and downs, your joys and sorrows, your successes and sins. He is waiting for you with open arms.

When you learn how to dwell in the shadow of the Almighty, you will discover life like you have never known it before. It is worth it to release the unhealthy fear of God that has been holding you back for so long.

It is more dangerous to live away from God's presence than in it. God is not scary. He is awesome and worthy of our praise. He is able to meet us where we are, forgive us, heal us and change us. I challenge you now to walk with God every day, unafraid, so that He can work in your life and bring to pass all He has called you to accomplish.

God is not against you; He is for you! Don't live out of an unhealthy fear of Him, always running and hiding. Fear God with love and worship and find joy and purpose in the shadow of His wings.

FEARLESS
LIVING

FEARLESS
LIVING
INTRO >>>

IT'S NOT EASY

"Well, no one said it would be easy. No one promised me a ride on angel wings." This line from my song "Energy" really says it all. As we have been talking about getting rid of our fears, I hope it didn't come across as an easy thing to do. Life is hard. There is no way around it. Even walking with God can be hard sometimes, but it is worth it to trust Him completely so that fear doesn't hold you back.

Fear is something we all struggle with, whether of failure, loneliness, man or even God. But there is help. You don't have to conquer fear alone. When the enemy attacks and tries to drag you down with fear, you have Someone to turn to who is more powerful than the enemy.

God wants you to move straight into your purpose so that you can live a fulfilling life. He is on your side and has made a way for you to have victory over the things that hold you back. Through Jesus, you can live fearlessly. In His name, you can finally live out the dreams and purposes in your heart.

I know you may feel weak or powerless to really get rid of all that you fear, but there is one more bit of truth I want to share, which I believe will give you the strength to triumph once and for all. Stay with me this last leg of our journey, and I know God will deliver you into fearless living.

FEARLESS
LIVING

QUESTION >>>

> WHAT DOES IT TAKE?

Do you have what it takes to get rid of fear? Do you know what kind of power you need to gain victory?

"Fearless" can be an intimidating word. If fear is common to all man, how can we ever expect to become "fearless"? Well, I'll tell you that it is not something we can achieve by ourselves. Past mistakes, failures and sins have made our hearts weak. Left to our own strength, we could never manage to get rid of all fear.

For us Christians, there is hope beyond our own strength. Maybe you have already experienced this power before. Have you ever encountered something so difficult, you didn't think you could make it through? Maybe it was a season of loneliness or failure. But then, did you make it? And did you come out the other side a stronger and better person?

If so, you already know what I am talking about. There is something else, Someone else inside of you who is armed and equipped to supply the energy and strength you lack. The Holy Spirit lives in you, moving and working every day, every minute.

When it comes to fear in your life, the Holy Spirit is the key, the force required for you to truly live fearlessly.

QUESTION

FEARLESS
LIVING

KEY >>>

POWER

# TAP INTO THE ENERGY

Later, I will share my song, "Energy," with you. It talks about how God's Spirit in our lives gives us the motivation and power to live in victory. No matter if you are held captive to the fear of loneliness, failure, man, God or anything else, God has given you everything you need to break those chains and charge forth into your destiny.

The Bible has so much to say about the role of the Spirit in our lives. He is God's love over us (Romans 5:5), our Teacher (John 16:13), Empowerer (Acts 1:8) and Equipper (1 Corinthians 12:1-11). If we ever hope to shake off the shackles that bind us, we need Him to be all of these things in our lives!

Think about it, when you are lonely or depressed, what do you need? The love of God. When you are deceived by the enemy, what do you need? A Teacher. When you are weak and unable to go on, what do you need? An Empowerer. And when you feel unqualified to do all that God has called you to do, what do you need? An Equipper.

The Holy Spirit is God's complete answer to our fears. And the wonderful thing about Him is . . . He already dwells inside of you! Second Peter 1:3 tells us that God has already given us everything we need for life and godliness, we just need to tap into it. Let's work back through the four fears we have already discussed and see how the Holy Spirit can take your hand and deliver you from them once and for all.

KEY

FEARLESS
LIVING

ECHO > > >

ENERGY TO OVERCOME THE FEAR OF FAILURE

No one wants to start something and then fail. We are all afraid of falling down! But the Bible says, "for though a righteous man falls seven times, he rises again . . ." (Proverbs 24:16). Failure is not in falling down; it is in not getting back up again! A righteous man, one who follows after God's heart, always gets up again.

We all make mistakes: "For all have sinned and fall short of the glory of God" (Romans 3:23). But when you do mess up, God does not look at your actions and call you a failure. No, God is most interested in the attitude of your heart (1 Samuel 16:7).

Success in God's eyes is a heart geared toward Him. Whatever you attempt, if you do so abiding in God's Word and trusting in the power of His Spirit, you will succeed. Even if the world tells you that you messed up, God will take your mistakes and turn them into muscle to make you stronger. "And we know that in all things God works for the good of those who love him, who have been called according to his purpose" (Romans 8:28).

Let me tell you something, you cannot fail in God's Kingdom when you abide by His Word (John 15:5). And to abide in the Word, you have to know the Word. As you read and understand the Bible, you will live out what it says and become like an arrow of light penetrating the darkness. Where there was only failure before, success will break through.

"'Not by might nor by power, but by my Spirit,' says the LORD Almighty" (Zechariah 4:6). Remember, the Holy Spirit is the energy you need to push through the fear of failure. He is the fighting spirit you need to get up again and again. Filled with the Holy Spirit, you can rule over failure by never giving up on doing what Jesus has told you to do.

God calls you a warrior, champion and overcomer. No matter how you feel or what is going on around you, you have to believe what He says about you. The difference between a champion and a second-placer is a passion and willingness to run to win. Friends, "Run in such a way as to get the prize" (1 Corinthians 9:24).

Don't let the fear of failure rule your life. Refuse to give up. Know the Word. Live the Word. Rely on the Spirit and run the race set before you with all your heart, mind, soul and strength.

FEARLESS LIVING

ECHO >>>

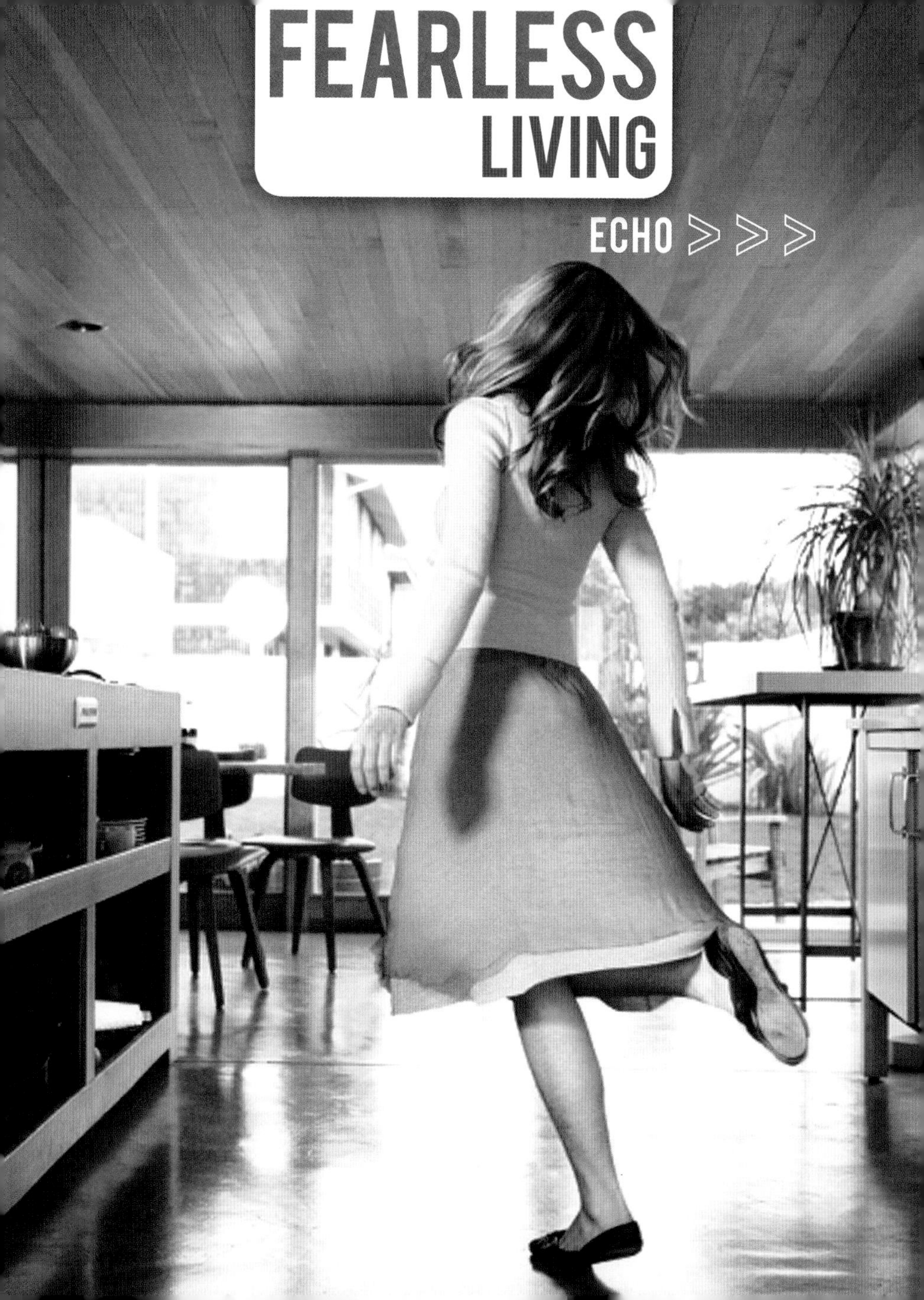

ENERGY TO OVERCOME THE FEAR OF LONELINESS

Loneliness is one of my favorite topics to talk about because it is surprisingly beautiful. Most people just don't understand it in light of its purpose. Where else but in solitude can you hear God's still, small voice so clearly and distinctly?

Where was Moses when God called to him from a burning bush to lead His people to deliverance? Alone in the desert. Where was Joseph when God trained him to become one of the greatest rulers in the world? Alone in prison. Where was David when God anointed him to be the next king of Israel? Alone with his sheep. And where did Jesus go to meet with His Father? To be alone.

God trained all of these men for their kingship through times of loneliness. According to Revelation 1:6, you and I are kings too. Through times of loneliness God wants to draw us to Himself so that we can step into the royal mission He has called us to.

If you fear being alone because you think it will take away your life, you need to shift your perspective. Instead of dreading loneliness, embrace it. Run to God and treasure alone time with Him. Choose to draw near to Him, hear His voice and discover His purposes for that season.

The Holy Spirit plays a key role in your kingship training during loneliness. As God's active presence in your life, He is the actual agent of change that molds you and shapes you to become the king God intended you to be. Again, it is the Holy Spirit who supplies the strength and energy to overcome your fear of loneliness and embrace it for all it can be in your life.

There was a time when I hated to be alone. Now that I have learned that I am never actually alone, that God through His Spirit is always with me, I love to be alone. In fact, I even ask God to give me times of solitude so that I can spend it with Him. Looking back, I see how God used those times to break me through to the next level.

You are a king, but you need to be trained. Let God create something beautiful out of the loneliness in your life. Allow the Holy Spirit to mold you in your kingship training.

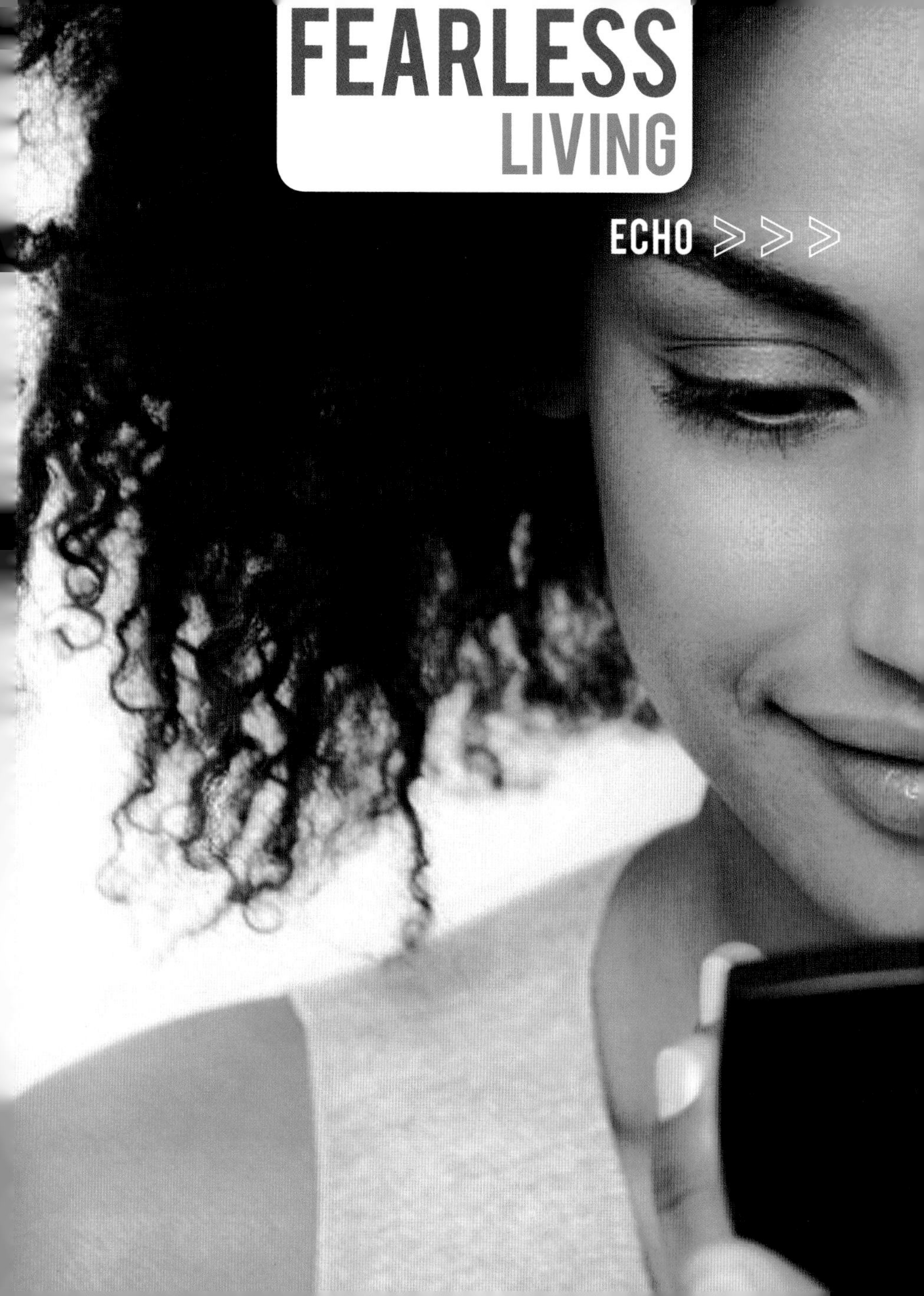
FEARLESS
LIVING
ECHO

> ENERGY TO OVERCOME THE FEAR OF MAN

Being afraid of man actually begins with a focus on self. As soon as you start to think, "I have to . . ." or "It is my job to . . ." you are placing your hope and trust in your own abilities. Then when you look at how others are doing, you instinctively try to measure up to their standards. That is when the fear of man kicks in.

God wants you to trust Him for all things. He wants to define your life's calling and show you the way to fulfill it. He wants to set the standard you live up to. When you fear man, you are robbed of the rewards of a faith-filled life and doomed to the limitations of man.

When you finally remove focus from yourself and place it instead on God, you will accomplish a very important command in Scripture: "Humble yourselves, therefore, under God's mighty hand . . ." And when you do humble yourself before God, you will find that He will "lift you up" (1 Peter 5:6). Only God can lift you up; you can't do that for yourself.

Friends, you have to believe in faith that no matter what others say, you will stand on God's promises. God's opinion is above man's. As the psalmist says, "In God I trust; I will not be afraid. What can man do to me?" (Psalm 56:11). Remember, we must respect and love all people, but we are to honor God above everything else.

As you learn to live according to God's promises and His calling, you will begin to stand out in the crowd. Man's standards won't matter to you anymore, and that will make you different. When others question what sets you apart, you can tell them that it is the Holy Spirit inside of you. You have the power of God at work within you, and that makes you special.

When the power of the Holy Spirit pulses through your body, you will know that it is not of you. When you feel His energy in your blood, you will know that God is alive in you. And if God is for you, who can be against you (Romans 8:31)? With God on your side and His Spirit dwelling within you, you have no reason to fear man.

FEARLESS
LIVING

ECHO >> >> >>

ENERGY TO OVERCOME THE FEAR OF GOD

From the depths of my heart, I wish you could understand how great it has been for me to serve the living God. I used to ski at a national level in my home country, and then I was a professional soccer player – my life has been so blessed. But still, nothing compares to walking with God Almighty.

Fearing God is about respecting and honoring Him, not being so afraid of His presence that you run away. He is your Father, and He is on your side. Running from God is running from joy, purpose, fulfillment and hope.

When you step into the boundaries God has set for your life, you will reach your potential faster and more efficiently. The enemy wants you to avoid those boundaries so that he can keep you from your passions and dreams. He will tell you that God gave you boundaries to make your life boring and difficult. But that is not true!

God knows that some things in life will only sidetrack you. He calls you to walk the narrow road, to avoid those hindrances so that you can move straight into your purpose.

You see, there is a copy of you running around. This copy is the you that everyone else says you should be. As long as you run from God, you will only be the copy of you.

The real you is who God created you to be. He gave you unique gifts, passions and experiences so that you could walk in His grand purpose for your life. He has given you His Word to show you what it means to live as the real you. Read it and discover all His promises to you for a blessed, abundant and free life. In the pages of Scripture, you will discover all that the real you can become.

If you spend your life trying to escape God's presence, you will never fully become the real you. Draw near to God. Love Him. Dwell in His perfect love that can drive out all of your fears. God wants you to reach further than you have ever reached and to bless more people. This is His purpose for you.

Don't be afraid of God. Don't run from Him. Run to Him.

FEARLESS
LIVING

NEXT STEP >>>

> YOU HAVE WHAT IT TAKES

If at one point you were discouraged at the thought of getting rid of all your fears, I hope now you have found strength.

The Holy Spirit is the energy, the power, all you need to live fearlessly, and the only way to have the Spirit is to have faith in Jesus. The Bible tells us that we are all sinners (Romans 3:23), but that Jesus has paid the price for our sins (1 John 2:2). The Bible tells us, "That if you confess with your mouth, 'Jesus is Lord,' and believe in your heart that God raised him from the dead, you will be saved" (Romans 10:9). Do you believe that Jesus died for your sins? If so, pray a prayer like this one:

"Jesus, I know you died for my sins and I believe God raised you from the dead. I want to know you like Eddie John is talking about. Please come into my heart."

If you prayed that prayer, you are saved and the power of the Holy Spirit has come on you. You can know God intimately and walk with Him every day. You can live without fear.

With Jesus as your Savior, God as your Father and the Holy Spirit as the energy flowing through your veins, you have everything you need to live fearlessly. I pray that all I have shared with you has put you on the path to conquering your fears and fully living out your destiny.

NEXT STEP

FEARLESS
LIVING

SONG >>>

ENERGY

I got so many questions stuck before my mind
I see so few solutions so I push them all behind
People ask me how I'm doing
I say I'm just fine
But deep inside there's a battle raging that is driving me completely wild

Well no one said it would be easy
No one promised me a ride on angel wings
But I've got the Holy Ghost inside me
Within I got all it takes to win

Cause I got so much energy in my blood
My heart is pumping with the beat of a drum
Forcing a flow, a river of peace through my veins
I know I found Thy Kingdom come

Life isn't easy I can tell you that for sure
Temptation lies behind every corner just waiting for an open door
But greater is He who lives in me than any power of this world
As long as I just keep my faith, there's no one that can

Well no one said it would be easy
No one promised me a ride on angel wings
But I've got the Holy Ghost inside me
Within I got all it takes to win

Cause I got so much energy in my blood
My heart is pumping with the beat of a drum
Forcing a flow, a river of peace through my veins
I know I found Thy Kingdom come

I'm not the type of man to give up easily
And I won't give up without a fight
But no one said it would be easy
No one promised me a ride on angel wings

Cause I got so much energy in my blood
My heart is pumping with the beat of a drum
Forcing a flow, a river of peace through my veins
I know I found Thy Kingdom come

SONG

FEARLESS
LIVING

PRAYER >>>

LORD, FILL US

Lord Jesus, we don't want fear to rule our lives. We want You to rule our lives. Thank You for the gift of Your Spirit. Fill us, fresh and full, so that we feel Your energy flowing through our bodies. By the power of Your Spirit, completely rid our lives of fear.

Father, if anyone reading this does not know You personally, draw them to Yourself by Your Spirit. If anyone still struggles with the fear of failure, give them Your fighting Spirit to get up time and again and accomplish Your calling on their lives. If anyone is held down by the fear of loneliness, remind them that they are never really alone. If anyone is defeated by the fear of man, I ask You to open their eyes to Your promises of success. And if anyone is running away from You, overwhelm them by the kindness of Your love.

Almighty God, bring us to freedom. Make all our dreams come true in You. We love You, Lord.

FEARLESS
LIVING

CHALLENGE >>>

> LIVE FEARLESSLY!

Your eyes have been opened to the enemy's weapons against you. He uses fear to hold you down and destroy your chance at living up to your potential. God has given you a calling and passion, deep in your heart, and He has equipped you with His power to accomplish all He has called you to do. Now it is up to you . . .

Abide in God's love through a vibrant relationship with Jesus Christ. Spend time with Him every day. Get to know Him better and draw close to Him when you are tempted to fear. Trust His Word for wisdom, and let it make your path straight.

Break the fear factors in your life. Let God's perfect love cast out your fears for good. Remember, you can do all things through Christ who gives you strength (Philippians 4:13). Destiny is calling. Now go and live fearlessly!

CHALLENGE